Saving Lake Superior

A Story of Environmental Action

by Wendy Wriston Adamson

Dillon Press, Inc.

Dillon Press, Inc., 500 South Third Street
Minneapolis, Minnesota 55415

Printed in the United States of America

Library of Congress Cataloging in Publication Data

Adamson, Wendy Wriston.
    Saving Lake Superior; a story of environmental action.
    Bibliography: p. 74
    SUMMARY: Traces the geologic and industrial history of
Lake Superior, the pollution of the lake, and steps being
taken to save it.
    1. Environmental protection — Superior, Lake — Citizen
participation. 2. Reserve Mining Company. [1. Environmental protection — Superior, Lake. 2. Superior, Lake] I. Title.
TD171.3.S9A3   363.6'09774'9   74-17351
ISBN 0-87518-138-4

CONTENTS

To Del

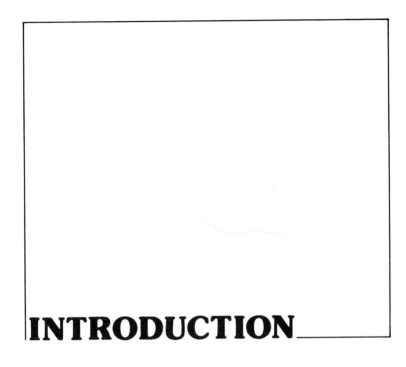

INTRODUCTION

The big ballroom at the Hotel Duluth was packed with people. It was the third day of testimony, and everyone was tired and stiff from sitting for so long. Scientists had testified. Lawyers had spoken. Learned professors had given their opinions. Industrial experts had presented long reports and complicated charts and graphs.

Walter Sve, a commercial fisherman from Split Rock, Minnesota, on the shore of Lake Superior, stood up. He explained that his father before him had fished along the shores of the great lake in the early part of the century. "When I was growing up, I just loved to hang over the side of the boat, my brother and I, and look down into the water. We would find chains lying on the bottom from back in the clipper days. I now have three children.

Today I can't take them out and show them what the lake bottom looks like."

Mr. Sve continued, "My dad had three big boats. You could troll the boat and look around the bottom for lake trout. Today you can't do that; you can't see that far." He went on to explain that he believed pollution had had a terrible effect on his fishing area, just off Split Rock. "In October, 1956, I caught 150 pounds (of herring) per net per day. By October, 1958, this had dropped to 48 pounds per net per day, and by 1959 it had dropped to 11 pounds per net per day." Mr. Sve said that he was a bit hesitant to speak before this large a crowd, especially as he had appeared at hearings before and nothing had come of them. But, he said, "I felt it was my patriotic duty to this great country of ours to come and make a statement, as we have this beautiful lake and it is being so wrongfully misused."[1]

Mr. Sve is just one of many thousands of citizens who love Lake Superior and want to protect it. He made the effort of coming to a government hearing that was full of experts, waiting patiently for many long hours for his turn to speak, so he could tell in his own way how he as one individual felt about the lake.

This is the story of Lake Superior, and how people who loved it banded together to try to save it. It is the story of a long, hard struggle which isn't over yet. It is a complicated story — because the issues cannot easily be separated into wrong and right, good and bad. It involves history, geology, ecology, economics, politics, and human fears and frailties. The story doesn't have a rosy ending, but it does give people hope that with hard work they *can* protect their earth.

Lake Superior is, indeed, worth protecting. Imagine a

Palisade Head on the North Shore of Lake Superior

lake with a surface area almost as large as the state of Maine, and bigger than Vermont, New Hampshire, Massachusetts, and Connecticut put together. Imagine a lake with 2,796 miles of shoreline — the distance between Los Angeles and New York City. When you stand on the shores of Lake Superior it is as though you were at the ocean. Surf pounds and crashes on the rocks. You can strain your eyes and see nothing but an endless flat horizon of water. Long sandy beaches with high dunes ring the lake. Dozens of sparkling cold waterfalls tumble into its waters. Dark pines and firs stand majestically on high craggy cliffs. Loons play along the shorelines, and deep below the surface, in icy dark reaches of the lake, fish and other underwater creatures move silently about.

Located right in the heart of the North American continent, Lake Superior is the westernmost of the chain of Great Lakes. Water flows from Lake Superior into Lake Huron, from there down into Lake Michigan and east into lakes Erie and Ontario, and then towards the Atlantic Ocean along the St. Lawrence Seaway. At the extreme western end of Lake Superior are the twin ports of Superior, Wisconsin, and Duluth, Minnesota, separated only by the St. Louis River emptying into the lake. At the eastern end are the famous Sault Sainte Marie falls, where Superior's waters rush downward into Lake Huron.

Lake Superior holds 3,000 cubic miles of water. If you could put it in a tank 1 mile wide and 1 mile high, it would stretch all the way across the United States. This represents about 12 percent of the entire world's supply of fresh water, and so it is very precious. One interesting thing to remember about Lake Superior is that scientists have calculated that it takes an unusually

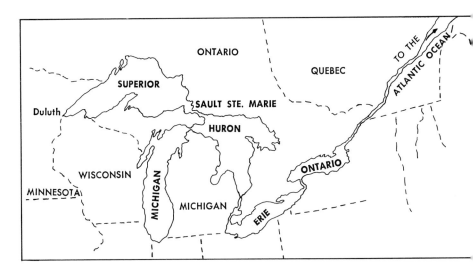

From Duluth to the Atlantic Ocean is some 2,300 miles by water. The chart below shows the comparative depths of the Great Lakes.

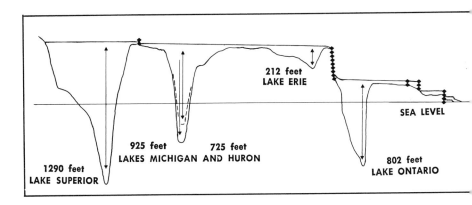

212 feet
LAKE ERIE

SEA LEVEL

925 feet   725 feet
LAKES MICHIGAN AND HURON

1290 feet
LAKE SUPERIOR

802 feet
LAKE ONTARIO

long period — about 500 years — to "flush" itself. Every so many years the water in any lake changes completely, just as the cells in a person's body change completely every 7 or so years. Lakes lose water primarily through evaporation, and they regain it through precipitation. Because Lake Superior is such a deep lake (at one point 1,290 feet), it has a relatively small surface area compared to its cubic feet of water. This means that evaporation takes place very slowly. In comparison, Lake Erie takes only about 35 years to flush itself. We shall see later the significance of this to Lake Superior's survival.

In order to understand some of the problems facing Lake Superior today, it is necessary to turn to the past, to see how the lake was formed and what influences man has had upon it. We shall explore the geological history of the Superior Basin, and then watch as Indians, explorers, lumbermen, and miners move across the lake's waters, settle on its shores, and alter its appearance.

1.

GEOLOGY

Indian legends say that Lake Superior was formed when giant beavers built dams at the Sault Sainte Marie on the eastern end of the lake (*Sault* means a falls or rapids in French). The beaver dams, according to legend, prevented the water from draining out into the other Great Lakes. The real story is even more interesting. Geologists have estimated that the development of the Lake Superior Basin took place over a period of several billion years. During most of this time, seas covered almost all of what is now Minnesota. Gradually these seas dried up and retreated. At least one billion years ago, volcanic eruptions in the area of the lake began, spewing out lava that covered the surrounding land. As the lava poured out, the crust of the earth lost its support and began to sink and eventually collapse, forming the large hole or basin which was to become the lake.

The Glacial Age

The Ice Age then brought sheets of glacial ice down from the north. As they advanced and retreated several times, their melt water began to fill the Superior Basin, and their movement dug out great areas in and around the lake. The lake we see today is primarily the evidence of the last large glacier, called the "Wisconsin Glaciation" which began about fifty thousand years ago. When the huge mass of ice finally retreated, about eleven thousand years ago, it left, where Lake Superior now stands, a much bigger, deeper lake called by geologists Glacial Lake Duluth.

The size of Glacial Lake Duluth must have been staggering! Geologists know that it was five or six hundred feet deeper than Superior, filling the Superior Basin to the brim and covering much of what is now dry land. During this period, streams flowing into the lake carried silt, sand, and gravel which were deposited along the shore, forming beaches. These beaches can still be seen today along the hills high above the city of Duluth, and they act as "time lines" to us. As the ice that was still retreating to the east and north gradually melted, it unplugged outlets for drainage, and the water level dropped. When the level remained at any one mark for a considerable period of time, another beach "time line" would form, and so we can follow the gradual retreat of the shoreline through thousands of years.

Since the glaciers eventually retreated eastward and northward, the greatest changes then taking place were

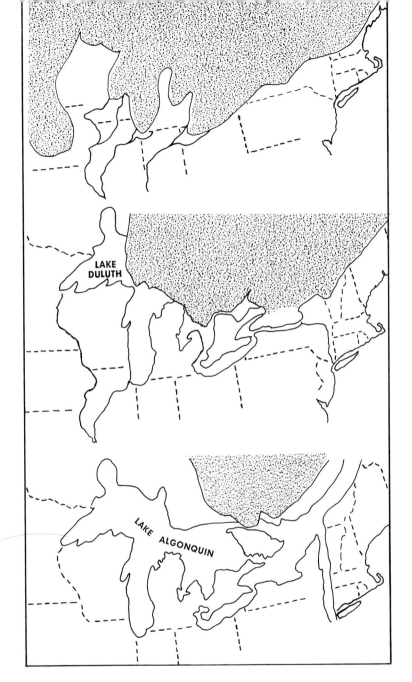

The Wisconsin Glaciation retreated to the north and east, leaving behind large bodies of water that eventually became the Great Lakes.

Beaches of Glacial Lake Duluth as seen today

at the eastern part of the lake. The drainage outlet at the Sault Sainte Marie was gouged out by the glacier, and the other Great Lakes, where ice was still melting, were formed. Eventually drainage into these lakes brought Lake Superior's level to about 100 feet below what it is today. Then, by about 5,000 years ago, the lake rose to its current level of 602 feet above sea level. This rise was caused primarily by changes in the drainage patterns into and out of the lake. The current level is maintained because, as water from streams and rivers all around the northern shore of the lake flow into it, an equal amount drains out through southern outlets, primarily through the Sault Sainte Marie, into the other Great Lakes, and eventually into the ocean.

Tilting of the Basin

Another phenomenon, which began thousands of years ago and is still occurring, is the tilting of the Lake Superior Basin. Scientists have observed that either the north side is rising, or the south side is sinking, or perhaps both. Horizontal beaches have become slanted, with their northern sides higher. On the south, valleys have filled with water; on the north shore, lakes and rivers now fall into the lake in waterfalls. As a result, few good harbors exist on the north shore of the lake.

The tilting has also resulted in an effect that could confuse the amateur geologist. The same "time line" of a certain period — those sandy beaches mentioned earlier — might be twenty-five feet above the shoreline on the north side of Lake Superior, and submerged twenty-five feet below the water on the south shore!

Scientists have speculated that if this tilting continues, it will eventually cause the lake to drain into the Mississippi River rather than into the other Great Lakes. This would radically change the face of North America. However, since the tilting rate is less than one half foot per century, this wouldn't happen until thousands of years in the future.

After learning the scientific facts about the formation of the great lake, it's still fun to listen to romantic interpretations of how Lake Superior was formed. Following is one such version, given by James H. Baker in a speech to the Minnesota Historical Society on January 24, 1879:

When it was, in what epoch of the world's great history, these grim masses of primitive rock in which this lake lies imbedded first lifted their basaltic scalps to the sky, the geologist himself cannot tell. When the waters went down, and the volcanic masses up, it matters not. Millions of years gaze at you from the grey cliffs which encircle this sea. And the same primitive upheaval spreads north, through realms as large as Europe, filled with wild lakes, roaring cataracts, rugged cliffs and impassable solitudes, in savage grandeur, to that frozen zone where the wild swan flies to his summer home. Everything about this lake is inspiring. More than a thousand miles from the sea, it reproduces in the heart of a continent the majesty and power of the "dark, deep, blue ocean." It is a sea, not a lake. It breeds storms and fogs and rain, like an ocean. It is an independent factor in the world's water system.[2]

2.

EARLY HISTORY

Historians have evidence that prehistoric man visited or lived on the south shore of Lake Superior. Copper knives, utensils, and weapons found near copper deposits have led them to speculate about the possibility of primitive mining operations. However, no definite conclusions have been reached as to how extensive this early culture was.

The Chippewa, or Ojibway, Indians were established on the lakeshore when the white man arrived. They survived by learning to live in harmony with nature. They ate fish from the lake and killed animals for meat. The skins and furs of the animals were used for clothing and shelter. Canoes were constructed from birch bark, and pine pitch was used to patch them. The Indians had

Grand Portage in 1857, *painting by Eastman Johnson, a
nineteenth-century American artist*

---

a strong love and respect for the land, and knew how to
use it wisely.

In the early seventeenth century, the famous French
explorer Samuel de Champlain sent an interpreter,
Ettiene Brulé, to live among the Indians and to explore
the country. Brulé was probably the first white man to
canoe into Lake Superior. By the middle of the century,
some fairly accurate maps of the area were drawn by
men who paddled the shores and walked the woods of the
lake.

No one knows for certain where the name Lake Superior originated. One story is that it refers to the French
phrase *le lac supérieur,* meaning simply the uppermost
lake in the Great Lakes chain. Other Frenchmen called
it Grand Lac, and the Chippewa gave it the name Kitchi-
Gammi, or Big Lake. It even appears on some early
French maps as Lac Tracy and Lac Condé, but these
names did not catch on. Somehow the name Lake Su-

perior stuck — it is easy to see why, since in every sense of the word it is a superior lake!

Among the early whites who came to Lake Superior, several groups stand out because they came with a purpose. When we consider the physical and mental discomforts they had to endure, it becomes obvious that without some strong mission they would never have undertaken such an effort.

Travel, mostly by canoe, was slow and clumsy, with long back-breaking portages, when canoes and supplies had to be carried through nearly impassable thick woods and underbrush, or up and down steep hills and ravines. Climate was unreliable even in the summer months, and Lake Superior storms could rival those on the ocean in suddenness and violence. And in winter months, of course, temperatures were below zero for long stretches, and lakes and rivers were frozen over.

Still another hardship was a tiny one — bugs! J. Elliot Cabot, on a scientific expedition on Lake Superior in 1848, wrote of one variety, after his party had already been plagued by mosquitoes for nights on end:

Today we made our first acquaintance with the genuine "black fly," a little insect resembling the common house fly, but darker on the back with white spots on the legs, and two-thirds as large. They are much quicker in their motions, and much more persevering in their attacks, than the mosquito, forcing their way into any crevice, for instance between the glove and coat-sleeve.[3]

Several days later:

Neither love of the picturesque nor the interests of science could tempt us into the woods, so terrible were the black flies.

This pest of flies, which all the way hither had confined our ramblings on shore pretty closely to the rocks and beach, and had been growing constantly worse and worse, here reached its climax . . . . We could only sit with folded hands, or employ ourselves in arranging specimens, and such other occupations as could be pursued in camp, and under the protection of a "smudge." One, whom scientific ardor tempted a little way up the river in a canoe, after water plants, came back a frightful spectacle, with blood-red rings around his eyes, his face bloody and covered with punctures.[4]

(A smudge, as you probably guessed, is a good smoky fire.) In some years there seemed to be no black flies, in others millions of them. No one knew why.

So with discouragements like the terrain, the climate, and the insects, only men with a firm reason and much dedication ventured into this wilderness in the early days. Who were they?

The Missionaries

Those with the most obvious reasons for coming were the Jesuit fathers who arrived in the middle of the seventeenth century. They were strongly committed to their task of spreading Christianity, and suffered greatly both from the physical hardships mentioned above and from the less-than-friendly reception they got from the Indians, who in many cases were fearful or resentful of Christianity. However, some missionaries found friends among the Chippewa. Bishop Frederick Baraga, who had a mission in Grand Portage, was one of the priests who came to be much loved and respected by the Indians.

In addition to spreading the Gospel, these men did some teaching, and they were the first to record descrip-

Winter on Lake Superior's shore

tions and histories of the region in any great detail. They spent many long winter evenings writing about what they saw and did, and to them we owe much of our knowledge about the early settlements on Lake Superior.

The French Explorers

The French explorers were a determined and daring group who came from eastern Canada and from France, and were commissioned by King Louis XIV to explore the land. Pierre Esprit Radisson and his brother Médard Chouard, whose title was Sieur des Groseilliers, were two of the earliest, and they immediately sent back word about the enormous potential for fur trade in the area. They soon formed an alliance with the Chippewa, and with their help were able to explore and chart the lake region. The Indians knew Lake Superior well, respected it, and were familiar with its many moods. They had already marked the best portages, learned where the best fishing places were, and discovered how to handle the dangerous waters. They had a great deal to teach the white man. While we can thank the missionaries for much written material about the area, we are grateful to the explorers for supplying us with many good maps and charts, even though by modern standards these maps were still quite inaccurate.

The Fur Traders

The fur traders were the first real "businessmen" of the lake. Men from the eastern United States and from Europe came with blankets, guns, and tobacco, which they traded with the Indians for furs, primarily beaver

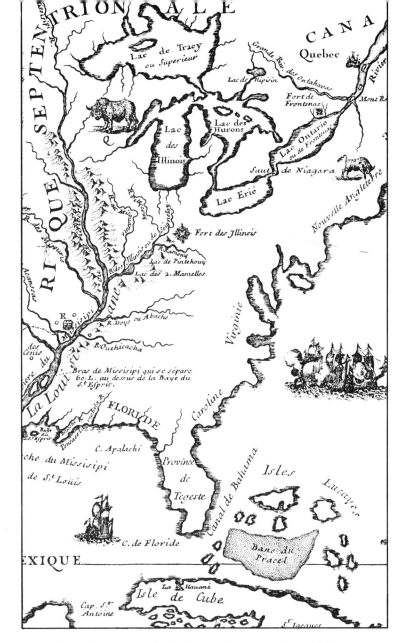

Map from A Journal of the Last Voyage Perform'd by Monsr. de la Sale, *published in Paris in 1713. Lake Superior is identified as Lac de Tracy.*

pelts. Beaver was in great demand all over Europe, where it was used most often for hats. For a long time it was the height of fashion to have a handsome hat of beaver fur, and almost everyone owned one. According to old journals of the early eighteenth century: "A single blanket was worth ten beaver skins; a common gun, twenty skins; a pound of powder, two; and a pound of shot, one."[5]

As the fur trade developed, the British used the Hudson's Bay routes to the north, while the French traveled primarily on the Great Lakes. Fur companies engaged in such fierce competition that they often resorted to robbery, violence, and murder. At first, competition was along national lines, with the French and the British trying to outdo each other. They destroyed each other's posts, pirated each other's goods, and shot each other's agents. After the French and Indian War, a treaty in 1763 gave Britain control of most of the fur trade. The British were smart enough, however, to recognize that the French were superior at doing the actual trading and transporting of furs, and immediately began to employ them.

The 1763 treaty was by no means an end to competition among fur traders. The Hudson's Bay Company and the Northwest Fur Company, both British, entered into a contest almost as fierce, though less violent, than the British-French one. The Hudson's Bay Company still did almost no trading on Lake Superior, until it merged with the Northwest Fur Company in 1821. After that they operated on the northern shores, while John Jacob Astor established the American Fur Company on the southern shores.

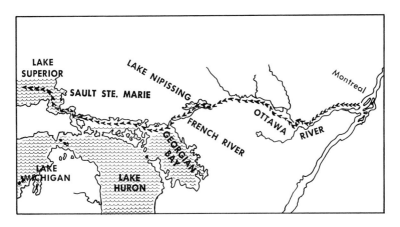

The voyageurs' route from Montreal to Lake Superior

The Voyageurs

The men employed by the fur companies to do the actual trading and transporting of goods were French Canadians called voyageurs. They usually traveled by canoe from Montreal to Grand Portage. Their route took them up the Ottawa River to Lake Nipissing, down French River to Georgian Bay, across the top of Lake Huron, up the Sault Sainte Marie to Superior, and finally to Grand Portage. The round trip usually took a year. They carried in manufactured goods and carried out furs. At Grand Portage they met with other voyageurs who had spent the winter in the area, traveling west through the lake chains and gathering furs from the Indians. The winter voyageurs felt they were quite superior to the traveling voyageurs, probably because they had to endure the severe climate while their brothers wintered in luxurious Montreal.

The voyageurs were a colorful group of men. Usually

they were short and had powerful arms and shoulders. No wonder. They could paddle their birchbark canoes, which held up to fifteen men, at a rate of sixty strokes a minute, and they could carry loads of two hundred pounds each over long, rough portages. They dressed in buckskins and silks of bright colors, with woven red sashes several yards long wound around their waists. These sashes and their tassled caps were their trademarks.

It was a beautiful sight when the voyageurs paddled into the harbor of Grand Portage during July, meeting with their counterparts who had spent the winter gathering furs. There was usually a week of festivities, with the men dancing and singing, engaging in various contests, and at night sleeping on the beaches under their overturned canoes.

The voyageurs soon became legends in the Great Lakes area. They were brave, extremely strong, loyal, and unusually good-natured, considering the hard work they did, sometimes traveling eighteen or twenty hours out of twenty-four. It is easy to wonder, reading all the glowing accounts of these men, if they ever woke up in the morning with bad tempers, or felt like being lazy and spending the day sleeping under their canoes. If so, history doesn't admit it. James Baker quotes one voyageur, who was over seventy, as boasting:

I could carry, paddle, walk and sing with any man I ever saw. I have been twenty-four years a canoe man and forty-one years in service; no portage was ever too long for me. Fifty songs could I sing. I have saved the lives of ten voyageurs. Have had twelve wives and six running dogs. I spent all my money in pleasure. Were I young again, I should spend my life the same way over. There is no life so happy as a voyageur's life.[6]

An 1867 drawing of voyageurs making a portage

Eighteenth-century Canadian voyageurs loading furs

3.

INDUSTRIAL DEVELOPMENT

During the eighteenth century the fur trade flourished on Lake Superior, and the area became somewhat settled and "civilized," as tiny trading posts developed into towns all along the shore. However, by the middle of the nineteenth century, the supply of beaver was exhausted and the trade died out. Modern industry was now about to begin, and the lake itself was to determine what these industries would be. The shoreland contained two major natural resources, wood and iron. Both of these existed in what seemed to be unlimited amounts.

Lumbering

Logging was a major industry on the lake from 1880 to

Lumber drivers breaking a jam

1925. Before it began, Lake Superior was surrounded by huge majestic trees — Norway and white pines, spruce, fir, cedars, and many hardwoods such as maples and birch. When J. Elliot Cabot canoed Lake Superior in the summer of 1848, he reported that the shoreline was entirely covered with these magnificent green forests. Half a century later, when the logging boom was over, there were no giants left.

During this period saw mills sprang up, towns developed along the shore, and shipping on the Great Lakes increased. Thousands of men traveled west from Europe and the eastern United States to work as lumberjacks. They lived in camps, working from dawn to dusk cutting and moving lumber. Their life was a difficult one. They slept on hay in cramped cabins and earned little salary. Nevertheless, they developed some of the same spirit and camaraderie of the voyageurs.

Another group of workers became known as the drivers or "river pigs." These were the men who would move timber down streams and rivers and into the lake. It was their job to walk on paths along the shores, guiding the logs. If the floating logs jammed, the drivers had to walk out on the turning logs, find the one causing the jam, and dislodge it. This required much skill, and "log rolling" eventually became a competitive sport for these men. Many falls into the icy water made the drivers' job a miserable one at times, but the men were usually paid higher wages than lumberjacks.

Almost overnight the Lake Superior area had prospered, but when the supply of lumber was exhausted, the industry died just as quickly. During the logging period the railroads began building short lines to haul some of the lumber from the inland camps to the Lake Superior shore, where it was then carried by boat down the Great Lakes. Almost all of the virgin growth along the lake was destroyed during the lumber boom, and what we see today is at least second and sometimes third growth. Most of the pines and fir did not grow back, but were replaced by hardwoods such as aspen, birch, and poplar. Even though these are lovely trees, they do not have the same primitive splendor of the evergreens, and the character of Lake Superior was definitely changed by the lumbering industry.

Mining

The Lake Superior Basin is a treasure house of minerals, of which iron is the most important. Copper, silver, and gold deposits have also been discovered. The proximity of these minerals to water (and thus easy transportation)

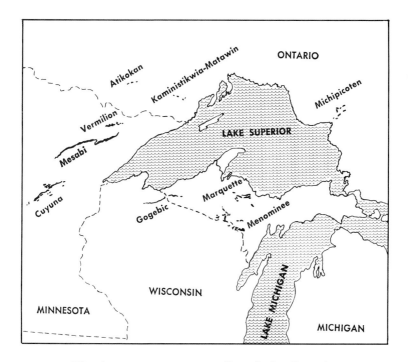

The iron ranges surrounding Lake Superior

made mining another industry that "boomed." But, unlike lumbering, mining is still going on. There are a number of iron ranges: the Atikokan, Kaministikwia-Matawin, and Michipicoten are in Canada; the Marquette, Menominee, Gogebic, Vermilion, Mesabi, and Cuyuna are in the United States. All are close to the lake.

The Mesabi Range alone is an enormously productive one. This range, which is about 110 miles long, was formed when iron was deposited from the seas covering Minnesota before the Volcanic Age. After the seas receded, this deposit was compressed into taconite, or iron-bearing rock. Over the years, rain water running through the rock layer gradually softened it, and dissolved out some of the sands and other worthless materials to leave a high concentration of iron.

The story of how the Merritt brothers of Duluth discovered the Mesabi Range is a fascinating one. Although people had been searching for iron in the area for years, it had not been located. The seven Merritt brothers had taken part in this search. One day in 1866, as two of them tramped over the hills north of Duluth, they suddenly took a good look at the earth beneath their feet. It was soft and crumbly and had a deep rich red color. In the past, iron had always been found in hard rocks. But suddenly it occurred to the men that *here* was what everyone was seeking, only in an unfamiliar form!

The famous red dirt of the Mesabi Range and the taconite deposits beneath it were tremendous finds, and an enormous industry developed in the Lake Superior area. It flourished until after World War II and is still in existence on a more limited scale today. Both surface and underground mining were done. Again, thousands of people arrived to work, as they had when lumbering began. The mining companies developed an extensive network of railroads to carry ore from the inland mines to the shore of Lake Superior and then east by ship.

Shipping

A third major industry, one that developed as a result of the two previously mentioned, was the shipping industry. If you look at the map on page 5, you can see that the Great Lakes offer a water passage all the way from Duluth to the Atlantic Ocean. In the old days, the eastern end of the route was the Erie Canal, which cut through

Open pit mining in the Cuyuna Range in Minnesota

A portion of the Duluth-Superior harbor at the westernmost tip of Lake Superior

New York State to the Hudson River. Today it is the St. Lawrence Seaway. Through this route, the entire central United States and Canada receive supplies such as coal and manufactured products from coastal areas and overseas, and Midwestern goods such as grain, lumber, and mining products are sent back out.

Not only heavy industry utilized the lake. For example, a tourist business grew up in the late nineteenth century, and the James J. Hill Company owned some cruise ships. Here is an excerpt from one of their pamphlets, written in 1896 to attract women to the Lake

Superior area. It is entitled "A Summer Cruise on Inland Seas via the Great Lakes to the West":

Duluth is a city of men. It has a population of 60,000, a large percentage of which is made up of rich, eligible bachelors. And yet, young ladies crowd to Eastern summer resorts, season after season, where there are not enough to make up a set of lanciers. In these days, when emancipated womanhood goes everywhere, why does she pass Duluth, the lair of the lonely but decidedly eligible bachelor?[7]

A twisted cedar, thought to be more than three hundred years old, on Superior's shore near Grand Portage

4.

ENVIRONMENTAL PROBLEMS

The story of how Lake Superior and its surroundings became civilized and industrialized is, in many ways, the story of our whole country, and for that matter of most of the world. During earlier centuries man had little idea that natural resources could be limited in supply. It seemed that there would always be more forests to cut, more minerals to extract and use, more clean drinking water to be found. And, in reverse, it didn't seem possible that people would ever lack space to dump trash, garbage, and industrial wastes.

The shores of Lake Superior were blessed with enormous wealth, as we have seen. And the lake itself was of the greatest value of all. It seemed for many years that there was little cause for concern. But now we have become painfully aware that this is not so.

Yet this realization did not come overnight in a brilliant flash. It grew gradually in the minds of many citizens — people from Minnesota, Wisconsin, and Michigan, as well as Canada. They looked to the East and saw the filthy, chemically poisoned water of Lake Erie. They realized that, to prevent the same degradation of *their* lake, they must begin now, and not in fifty or a hundred years when it would be too late. Time was particularly important to Lake Superior, because, as we have mentioned, almost five hundred years are needed to flush it and clean up any damage man has done. This responsibility was not to be taken lightly.

Citizens began to look at some of the problems Lake Superior faced. The more people studied them, the less simple the solutions seemed. The problems were made worse by the fact that three states, Michigan, Wisconsin, and Minnesota, as well as a Canadian province, Ontario, all own part of the shoreline. Three states, one province, and two countries were involved. How many hundreds of counties, towns, and municipalities? There were literally several hundred governmental bodies and agencies whose decisions affected the lake in some way. The bureaucratic hurdles alone seemed insurmountable.

Basically, there are four major physical threats to Lake Superior itself. Each of them represents a different danger and has different solutions.

Oil Tankers

Every year, thousands of boats come in to the twin port of Duluth-Superior carrying goods such as manufactured materials and coal, and head out with Midwestern products such as ores and grains. Small amounts of oil and oil products are also shipped out of Lake Superior, and the amounts are likely to increase. For example, in late 1973 the Lakehead Pipe Line Company announced plans to begin shipping over six million barrels of refined petroleum from Superior, Wisconsin, to other Great Lakes ports on an annual basis, beginning in 1975. The oil travels to Superior from Canada via a pipeline. When the operation is going full-scale it will involve twelve million barrels annually.

We have all read about enormous oil spills in the oceans, spills that leave shorelines covered with the sticky substance for months and years, killing animals, birds, and fish, devastating the tourist and fishing industries, and making boating and swimming impossible. Oil tankers are very fragile. They are extremely long and narrow, and break apart relatively easily in strong waves. Off England's coast, for example, a tanker named the *Torrey Canyon* disintegrated in rough seas, and thousands of gallons of oil spread in a slick across the water, covering rocks and beaches with a deadly scum. The same could happen on Lake Superior, which is well known for its storms and fogs.

Shipping oil anywhere is a calculated risk man takes, with the environment at stake. It is essential that if oil shipments are to be continued and even increased on Lake Superior, the standards for construction of tankers be raised and methods of coping with weather and other natural hazards be improved to a great degree.

Sewage

Almost one hundred cities, towns, and districts dump

their sewage directly into Lake Superior. Some of this sewage has been exposed to modern treatment methods, but in many cases only the most simple processes are used, and many harmful bacteria go right into the water. This constitutes a major health hazard, particularly as the lake is used as drinking water by thousands of people.

Today, federal water quality standards are helping. The guidelines for developing these standards are contained in various United States laws, particularly in the Federal Water Pollution Control Act Amendments of 1972. These amendments list specific actions that must be taken by federal, state, and local governments and industries to clean up the nation's waters. If the actions are not completed by certain deadlines, the Environmental Protection Agency has the power to step in and take direct action. So all of the towns on the United States side of the lake are being forced to upgrade their sewage treatment facilities in order to meet federal and state standards. But only with uniform United States-Canadian standards, and then strict enforcement of these standards, will this problem be completely solved.

Not only do municipalities dump waste into the lake, but there has also been widespread seepage from cabins and resorts which are built so close to the shoreline that their pipelines or septic tanks leak into the lake. In the future, no construction will be allowed so close to the shoreline, and those buildings already there must improve their facilities so that pollution does not occur.

Erosion

Erosion is sometimes due to man's misuse of the land and sometimes due to nature. When the lumbering was

Turbid regions of western Lake Superior, resulting from erosion, determined by ERTS (Earth Resources Technology Satellite) remote sensing during September, 1973

being done and forests along the lake were "clear-cut" (that is, every tree was cut down), a certain amount of erosion took place, and silt and dirt were washed into the lake in large quantities. But as new growth appeared, this problem took care of itself.

The major instance of erosion on the lake now is found along the shore of northwestern Wisconsin, where red clay is being washed into the lake in large quantities. The color spreads far out into the water, and it is presenting a threat to life in trout streams along the shore, and to aquatic life of the lake itself. The erosion has been taking place for centuries and is primarily caused by nature. But man has made the problem worse by constructing highways and buildings along the shore and by experimenting with raising the level of the lake. Scientists and engineers are working on ways to reduce the erosion, and a series of retaining walls or dikes may be the only final answer.

Industrial Pollution

More than sixty industries discharge their industrial wastes into the lake. As we shall see, the activities of the iron industry, and in particular of Reserve Mining Company, were what sparked the citizens of the area to try to preserve the quality of the lake. Other industries include large paper mills located on the Canadian side of the lake and on the St. Louis River that flows into Lake Superior at Duluth, and chemical companies in both the United States and Canada. One chemical company recently stopped dumping its chemical effluents into Boyd Creek in Barksdale, Wisconsin.

There is speculation, too, about new industries to be built on the shore. For example, there has been some talk about a nuclear materials plant to be built on the Knife River in Minnesota, just off the lake. If new industries are built, uniform standards must be agreed upon and then enforced if further industrial pollution is to be avoided.

These and other problems faced the citizens of the Lake Superior area when they were mobilized in the late 1960s by one major issue, that of the operation of the Reserve Mining Company at Silver Bay, Minnesota. It took a major problem to get people moving in one direction, and as we shall see in the next chapter, Reserve Mining supplied it.

5.

THE MODERN MINING INDUSTRY

The iron industry thrived in Minnesota until a few years after World War II. But by then most of the easily extractable iron had been taken, and open pit and underground mines alike began to close down. In fact, much of the area became economically depressed, and unemployment ran high. Since the Lake Superior area relied so heavily on one industry and on one natural resource, when iron became less available and mining less profitable, many people suffered. Whole towns in the Mesabi Range area were full of men and women without jobs, families without money, stores without customers. Many people left for larger cities and jobs in other parts of the country.

Today's taconite industry is a comeback from this

depression. Taconite is a very hard rock that contains about 30 percent iron. For a long time this iron had been considered unrecoverable. But in 1948, Edward W. Davis perfected methods of extracting iron from the taconite ores. This was a major breakthrough, because taconite ores were still plentiful in the area. The Davis process involves shooting streams of burning kerosene and icy water alternately at the rock. The sudden change in temperature cracks the taconite, and then it can be blasted into chunks. The taconite industry began in the early 1950s to mine the still vast, if less accessible, resources of the Mesabi Range. The industry is considered a lifesaver to many of the surrounding towns, restoring their ability to function as healthy communities.

The Reserve Mining Company

Reserve Mining has two operations, one at Babbitt, Minnesota (inland), and the other at Silver Bay. The ore is mined at Babbitt by means of the Davis process, and then it is loaded into railroad cars and shipped down to Silver Bay, a distance of forty-seven miles. At Silver Bay, taconite is extracted from the ore. It is a simple process. The ore is ground up until it consists of particles finer than flour. Then magnets are used to separate the taconite from the grains of silica and other undesirable materials. The usable taconite is compressed into pellets, the product of the plant. An enormous amount of water is involved in this process for washing and moving the materials. In fact, 700 million gallons of Lake Superior water go through Reserve's plant every day. And when the water is returned daily to the lake, it carries with it 67,000 tons of taconite tailings, tiny particles of iron,

Taconite ore being shipped in railroad cars from Babbitt to
Silver Bay

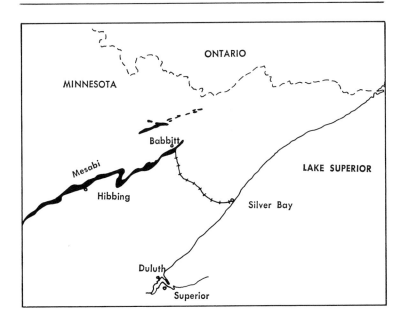

Aerial view of Reserve's Silver Bay plant, showing the delta created by the taconite tailings

silicates, and other minerals. Imagine — 67,000 tons of tailings dumped into the lake every day!

Reserve Mining Company did not do this dumping without permission or official sanction. In 1947 they were granted a permit by the state of Minnesota to do it. They also received a federal permit from the U. S. Army Corps of Engineers. At that time there was little opposition to the idea, although one far-sighted official stated, "It is my opinion that the deposition of the tailings in the waters of Lake Superior will be harmful to aquatic values, and may eventually cause a reduction in the supply of lake trout, whitefish, and lake herring by destroying their food supply and the covering of their spawning ground by depositing silt from the tailings on all such areas."[8] But to most people, the idea of dumping seemed safe enough at first. The tailings appeared much like ordinary sand, and were expected to settle on the bottom of the lake within a nine-square-mile area around the plant — a relatively small area indeed.

It is interesting to note that other taconite plants in Minnesota, such as the Erie Mining Company, installed on-land facilities for the disposal of their tailings, thus making their operations more expensive than Reserve's. In effect, Reserve was able to make a bigger profit on its operations because it enjoyed the privilege of dumping its waste into the lake, and thus did not have to build or maintain on-land facilities.

Late in the 1960s the company prepared to ask for a renewal of the Corps of Engineers' permit to dump. Meanwhile, however, observers had noticed changes in the lake, some of which seemed related to the taconite dumping. For example, a good deal of discoloration was noticed, including what is called "green water" — large patches of water with a milky-green hue. This was found down-current from Reserve, and was believed to be caused by taconite tailings suspended in the water.

In 1968, a Taconite Study Group made up of five agencies within the U.S. Department of the Interior did a study on the dumping and concluded that the procedure *was* harmful to the lake. Charles Stoddard was the Federal Water Pollution Control Administration official who was largely responsible for the report, called *Special Report on Water Quality of Lake Superior in the Vicinity of Silver Bay, Minnesota*. Some of the most important conclusions of the report were:

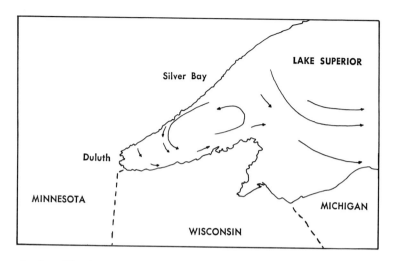

A simplified diagram of the general water currents in the western end of Lake Superior

• Of the 67,000 tons of taconite wastes dumped daily, over 5 tons consist of particles less than 4 microns in diameter. (One micron equals 1/25,400 of an inch, and the smallest particle the eye can see is about 40 microns.) Because particles this small are so light in weight they will stay in suspension for a long time. The large quantity of suspended particles causes the "green water" effect.

• Currents in the lake, which travel southwest at this point, curving around at Duluth-Superior and traveling up the Wisconsin shore, are capable of carrying these suspended particles 9 miles per day. (The agreed-upon limit for the tailings, remember, was a 9-mile-square area around Silver Bay.) It was to come out in a federal court in 1974 that 600 square miles of lake bottom had been covered with the tailings, and that in all 1,000 square miles had been affected. Tailings were found as far away as the Wisconsin shores.

• Studies in 1968 showed that water in the Silver Bay vicinity contained aluminum, lead, copper, zinc, cadmium, and nickel in amounts considered harmful to aquatic life.

• Bottom fish-food organisms were reduced where the tailings settled. This means less for fish to feed upon. Later studies were to show that the fish population was significantly altered. (Here one can look back to the fisherman Walter Sve and understand why he was so upset.)

• Also affecting aquatic life in Lake Superior was an increase in turbidity, or cloudiness, of the water. The suspended particles in the water cause the water to become murkier and less transparent. Consequently less light can reach the life on the bottom of the lake.

The results of the "Stoddard Report" were so controversial that many people dismissed the report as not really official, although no one was able to point to any specific errors in the entire publication.

6.

THE
CITIZENS
ORGANIZE

Prompted by the Stoddard Report and citizen response, Interior Secretary Udall called a Federal-State Conference on Lake Superior to be held in Duluth on May 13-15, 1969. The conference was one of the most exciting ones ever held in that area of the country, for reasons that we shall see. But first, it is important to note what the citizens had been doing before the conference took place.

There were people who lived along the lakeshore in Minnesota, Wisconsin, and Michigan who were aware of environmental issues and wanted to be sure that whatever decisions were made, someone would speak up for the lake. These people came from little towns like Beaver Bay and Two Harbors along Minnesota's majestic

The shore near Grand Marais, Minnesota

North Shore. They came from the beautiful scenic villages on Wisconsin's South Shore. And many were from the forests and meadows of Michigan's Upper Peninsula. In addition, citizens of the westernmost point of the lake, the twin ports of Duluth-Superior, had a vital interest in what was going to happen. Even people who did not live on the lake, but visited it in the summer and appreciated its beauty and fragility — people from as far away as Alabama and California — wanted to be heard.

So early in 1969 they got together and said, in effect, "If we form a group and conduct a real information campaign about the lake, maybe someone will listen to us." They believed that only if citizens let the government know how they feel about an issue, will the government be responsive to their demands. Chapters of the Save Lake Superior Association (SLSA) were formed that spring, and hundreds, and eventually thousands, of people joined. They held programs, slide shows, and lectures about Lake Superior. They spoke on local radio shows. They wrote articles for newspapers and magazines. They distributed thousands of buttons and bumper stickers, trying to make everyone aware of the danger the lake was in.

And most important, they told people about the conference that was coming up in May and encouraged everyone to come and stand up and speak about the lake. They said, "You don't have to be an expert to come and be heard. This question is too important to be left only to the experts. We should listen to what they have to say, because it helps us make our decisions. But we, as citizens, must make our own decisions, and then we must tell them to our representatives, if the government is to take the action we think best."

Students for Saving Lake Superior

At Ashland High School on Wisconsin's Superior shoreline, a group of students, who wanted their voices heard in the debate too, organized the Students for Saving Lake Superior (SSLS). In order to bring the issue to public attention, they obtained the use of several billboards in the Ashland area, which they painted with such slogans as "Let's Keep Superior Superior."

They gathered information on the activities of several industries on the lake, including the DuPont Company plant that was close by, and then met with officials of the companies to discuss what could be done to lessen industrial pollution. Because they had carefully studied all sides of the issues, and because they obviously were

SSLS members demonstrating at the 1969 Duluth conference

not operating for any personal gain, they became a significant and formidable force, and they gained the respect of the companies and the community.

The SSLS members came to the conference in Duluth in a schoolbus, bringing placards with slogans about protecting the lake. They presented a statement at the conference. A Duluth newspaper wrote a critical article about them, asking if such young people shouldn't be in school on a weekday, getting an education. SSLS supporters, including teachers from their school, responded that they knew of nothing more educational than this experience. Some weeks later the Duluth paper retracted its criticism. Meanwhile, even national publications such as *Time* magazine took notice of the activities of the group.

The students had successfully demonstrated that a young person need not wait until he or she has graduated from college or begun a career or reached a certain age before having an impact on decision making. They had succeeded in educating many people and in making themselves heard on an issue of national importance.

So, thanks to the encouragement and work of the Save Lake Superior Association and the Students for Saving Lake Superior, dozens of citizens clubs and organizations, many of which had never taken an official position on an environmental issue before, held meetings. They discussed the question of Reserve Mining's taconite tailings late into the night, and voted whether or not to send representatives to the conference in Duluth, and if so, what these representatives should say.

The Conference

On the morning of May 13, 1969, there were peaceful demonstrations outside of the Hotel Duluth, as people displayed signs about saving the lake. Inside, more than 600 people crowded into the brightly lit ballroom. The SLSA had arranged for the presentation of over a hundred statements from interested citizens, including conservationists, fishermen, scientists, teachers, students, and other people who loved the lake. This was democracy in action! The citizens were surprised and proud that so many of them had turned out to show they had the courage of their convictions.

Some of the many groups represented were the Sierra Club, the Wisconsin Wildlife Federation, the Izaak Wal-

Inside the ballroom of the Hotel Duluth during the conference

---

ton League, the U.S. Steel Workers of America (AFL-CIO) Local 5296, the League of Women Voters, Students for Environmental Defense, Minnesota Federation of Labor, and the United Northern Sportsmen of Duluth. The government officials present were also surprised that so many citizens had taken an interest, and the representatives of Reserve Mining Company were a bit apprehensive, no doubt, at such a strong turnout.

Here are some of the comments heard during those three days:

Senator Gaylord Nelson, U.S. Senator from Wisconsin
It is time we said: No one has a right to pollute the air, the water, the land. It belongs to us all and must not be used

for the special benefit of any community or company or individual.[9]

Richard J. Thorpe, Chairman, North Star Chapter, Sierra Club
The lake is a major national resource. The fact that it borders on only three of the fifty states makes it mandatory that these states, and the Federal Government, act as trustees for the benefit of the citizens of all the states and exert every effort to preserve Lake Superior in its present relatively unspoiled state.[10]

Milton Pelletier, United Northern Sportsmen Club, Duluth
We believe that the habits of a nation will finally determine its destiny. If we choose to pollute our waters, however it may be justified, or to allow our land to erode or to bury our country under tons of litter, or to allow other natural resources to be plundered, we are heading toward ruin and no amount of money will repair the damage.

We believe that every individual has a personal and continuing responsibility and an equity in all our natural resources, including water — but that there is, indeed, a much heavier responsibility upon those elected and appointed public servants charged with cleaning up our environment.

We believe that land or water ownership is merely a life tenure or custodianship to be passed on to succeeding generations, and that such ownership or custodianship does not carry with it the divine right to destroy.

We believe that everyone must have a reverence for the land and water and its fruits not based on profit motive. And any other course leads to exploitation and destruction, as we have learned, to our sorrow.

We know by very bitter experience how even a little pollution is prone to collect in unexpected places and manifest itself in some very unpleasant ways. Lake Superior, for all its vast area, depth and coldness of water, is most assuredly not immune to the ills that have served to cause such havoc in so many other lakes.[11]

Edward M. Brigham III, National Audubon Society of Michigan

I urge this conference to call for a halt to the dangerous "ecological brinkmanship" that says "let's wait, there is not enough evidence yet." Our system of law says that a man is innocent unless guilt is established beyond reasonable doubt. This same code cannot apply to pollutants and polluters.[12]

Mr. Brigham's provocative statement does not mean that people should be punished for crimes before they have a trial. But he is saying, in effect, if you saw a woman putting arsenic in her husband's coffee every morning, you would not wait until the husband were dead to take action. You, or the lawful authorities, would stop her. Then, if she could prove this was not a harmful action, she could continue. It is up to citizens to insist on pollution standards that will cause the potential polluter to prove *in advance* that it will do no harm to the lake. It is not satisfactory to let him pollute until there is certain, but also irreparable, damage.

Lawrence D. Downing, a lawyer from Rochester, Minnesota

I have traveled the north shore of Lake Superior by highway many, many times and at all times of the year; I have been on Lake Superior's north shore waters in boats ranging in size from a canoe up to the motor vessel *Winonah,* which runs daily from Grand Portage, Minnesota, to Isle Royale and I have occasionally even plunged into Lake Superior's frigid waters for a swim following a sauna.

Over the years I have watched the construction and operation of the Reserve Mining Company's taconite plant at Silver Bay, Minnesota — first with interest, then with growing concern and now with genuine alarm, even panic. I can recall the beautiful little bay and tiny islands that constitute the site of the Reserve Mining Company's taconite plant. I vividly remember the journey past the site after commencement of operation when I first noted a milky green water in the bay instead of the formerly beautiful clear blue. Now the sickening milky green color is spreading out into the body of the lake for several miles up and down the shore. It has even been reported that tailing residues have been detected across the lake on the Wisconsin shore. I have taken home movies of the area to display to my friends, who remember the former beautiful appearance of the water, the tragedy that is taking place in the name of "good business," "iron ore industry," and "additional tax revenue." I should have liked each and every member attending this conference to have seen the look on my five-year-old daughter's face as we moved from the mining company's Silver Bay look-out site for tourists to another spot where we could actually see the thousands of tons of tailings spreading out into our — mine and yours — lake.[13]

Some scientists at the hearing testified that the "aging" of Lake Superior had been greatly accelerated by the tailings. Most lakes are in the process of aging: they eventually become marshes, which then dry up and are replaced by land. Part of this process involves the growth of algae in the water, which use up available oxygen and therefore make existence difficult for fish and other organisms. A lake the size of Superior could be expected to complete the process of aging only over millions of years, if left to itself. However, included in the 67,000 tons of tailings dumped daily by Reserve Mining is approximately 51,500 pounds of phosphorous and 629,-000 pounds of manganese, both of which act as nutrients to speed the growth of algae. Studies showed that downstream from Silver Bay algae were growing at tremendous rates. One scientist stated that in twenty years the lake had aged hundreds of years in this area.

Not everyone agreed that the dumping of taconite tailings should stop. Reserve Mining Company appeared with dozens of consultants who presented long, thorough reports justifying the plant's activities. They maintained that there was not enough evidence to prove that the dumping was doing any harm. They also pointed out all the good the company had done for the area, building homes for the employees, financing schools and health clinics for their workers in Silver Bay and Babbitt, and paying taxes to the state of Minnesota.

One of the most vocal groups at the hearing was the body of people employed directly at Reserve, or indirectly by the two towns that house the workers. The company has claimed that if they are forced to change to on-land disposal of taconite tailings, it would be too expensive and they would be forced to close down the plant, leaving 3,000 people unemployed. The threat of closing is regarded by many people as nothing more than that — blackmail by the company to avoid changing its operation. (These people note that the other taconite plants with whom Reserve competes have disposed on land for years and presumably still found their business profitable.) But to the workers, their families, and others in the two towns, Reserve's threat is a serious one, and it affects their very future. They remember the times of depression in many of Minnesota's old mining towns. Naturally they do not wish to be left without employment, and therefore many people from these two towns came to the conference to plead that permission to dump be continued, and that the plant be allowed to function as it had for twenty-five years.

Their pleas were heard and taken seriously by everyone. No one, not even the most vigorous opponent of Reserve Mining Company's operations, wants these people to be left without jobs. This is a sad example of what happens if a town grows up around and depends upon any one industry exclusively — if the industry dies for any reason, the entire town is destined to die.

However, studies done on the cost of changing to on-land disposal have shown that Reserve and its two parent companies, Republic Steel and Armco, could absorb the cost of the transition and still continue to make a profit. (It has been stated in court that their current profit is $60,000 per day on the Reserve operation.) So in this case, the "danger" to the employees seems to be a manufactured one, really a weapon the company is using to avoid compliance with the law. It must be remembered, too, that for twenty-five years Reserve operated at an enormous economic advantage compared with the other taconite plants that were disposing on land.

7.

SLOW PROGRESS

The May 1969 hearings were just the beginning of the citizens' struggle to save Lake Superior. During the next several years three more enforcement conferences were held. Numerous studies were done by Reserve Mining Company, by the Federal Water Quality Laboratory in Duluth, by the state of Minnesota, and by private citizens. The debate went on and on, and an enormous body of evidence grew supporting the citizens' contention that the taconite tailings were harming the lake. Government officials were at times reluctant to take action, but citizen pressure continued to build.

In 1971, the U.S. Environmental Protection Agency finally issued an order that Reserve must stop the dumping. This was a monumental order, but it was by no means the end of the controversy. From here it went to the courts. A trial began on August 1, 1973, which was to become the longest trial in Minnesota history, and the longest environmental trial in the history of the nation. The United States Government filed the suit against Reserve. The states of Michigan, Wisconsin, and Minnesota, and environmental groups such as the Save Lake Superior Association and the Northern Environmental Council, became intervenors in the case, entering the suit on the side of the government.

In the midst of the long legal struggle that ensued, another dramatic event occurred in Duluth which made the outcome of the trial more important, and focused worldwide attention on Lake Superior.

The Asbestos Question

Testifying before the International Joint Commission in December, 1973, Arlene Lehto, chairwoman of the Save Lake Superior Association, suggested that the silicate cummingtonite, which travels as part of the taconite tailings, looked and acted suspiciously like asbestos, a known cancer-causing substance. Although many at the hearing felt that Mrs. Lehto was just trying another scare tactic, subsequent studies by state and federal agencies proved she was indeed correct. This meant that approximately 150,000 people in the Lake Superior area had been drinking water containing asbestos for at least fifteen years. (Lake Superior is the source of water for most of the residents near its shores.) Furthermore, it was established that Reserve Mining was emitting asbestos into the air around the plant, and that asbestos levels in the air of Silver Bay were dangerously high.

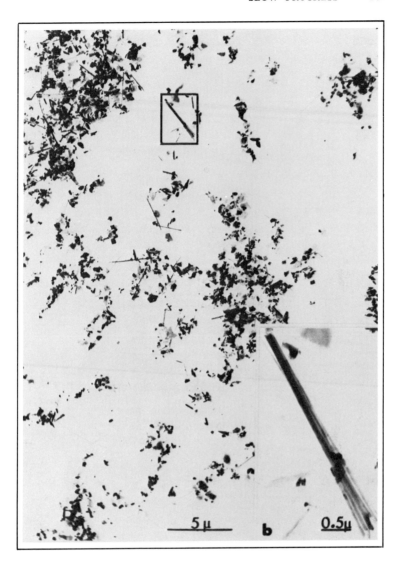

Electron micrograph of taconite tailings from Reserve Mining Company. Inset in lower right shows a higher magnification of an asbestiform amphibole fiber bundle. (0.5μ equals 0.00002 inches)

Asbestos can cause a number of physical ills. When inhaled, the particles often lodge in the mucous membranes surrounding the lungs, and they are impossible to remove. This results in the condition known as asbestosis, which causes increasingly severe coughing and difficulty in breathing. This disease was first recognized in the 1920s, but not until years later did anyone realize how widespread it was and how serious it could be.

In 1957, Dr. J. Christopher Wagner, a South African pathologist, discovered a high incidence of a previously rare form of cancer, called mesothelioma, among his patients. Mesothelioma is a condition which affects the membrane that surrounds the lungs or the membrane that lines the abdominal cavity. This kind of cancer is completely inoperable and always fatal. Since asbestos fibers were found in the bodies of many of his patients, Dr. Wagner was able to draw the conclusion that exposure to asbestos dust had some significance, perhaps causing the mesothelioma.

In 1964, Dr. Irvin Selikoff, of the Mount Sinai School of Medicine in New York, established that an extremely high percentage of asbestos workers were developing asbestosis and then mesothelioma. He noticed a most significant and frightening fact — that the two conditions did not appear until a period of twenty years or so after exposure to asbestos! This did not mean that the diseases had not started until then, but that they were not detectable for twenty or thirty years. Thus the high rate of illness in World War II and postwar workers from the New York shipyards, where Dr. Selikoff did his study, was not discovered until the 1960s. Since Reserve Mining began large-scale dumping in the mid-1950s, and then refined its crushing process in the mid-1960s to produce even finer particles, any cases of asbestosis and mesothelioma would not become evident for some time yet.

There is no guarantee that the disease will affect large numbers of citizens. Scientists and doctors hope that there may be something different about the Lake Superior situation that will make the comparison to the New York asbestos workers invalid. The American Cancer Society has begun a massive study in the Lake Superior area. But there is still no answer to the question of whether Reserve's operation is harmful. And while there is *any* reasonable doubt as to its safety, experts and citizens alike argue, shouldn't we take all possible precautions and stop the dumping until we know? Although this will not help the present condition of the water, it would at least stop further degradation. In addition, public health officials recommended that people drink bottled water from some other source than the lake. Imagine having to drink bottled water when you live on the shores of the largest body of fresh water in the world!

The Trial and After

On April 20, 1974, after 146 days of trial which included testimony from more than 100 witnesses, more than 1,600 exhibits, and more than 19,000 pages of transcript, Federal District Judge Miles Lord made a historic ruling. He listed the following findings of fact:

Reserve, acting as an instrumentality and agent for Armco and Republic, discharges large amounts of minute amphibole fibers into Lake Superior and into the air of Silver Bay daily.

The particles, when deposited into the water, are dispersed throughout Lake Superior and into Wisconsin and Michigan.

Exposure to these fibers can produce asbestosis, meso-thelioma, and cancer of the lung, gastrointestinal tract, and larynx.

The discharge into the air substantially endangers the health of the people of Silver Bay and surrounding communities as far away as the eastern shore of Wisconsin.

The discharge into the water substantially endangers the health of the people who procure their drinking water from the western arm of Lake Superior, including the communities of Beaver Bay, Two Harbors, Cloquet, and Duluth in Minnesota; and Superior, in Wisconsin.

The ruling goes on to list specific provisions of the Federal Water Pollution Control Act which are being violated, as well as state regulations. Then it says:

It has been clearly established in this case that Reserve's discharge creates a serious health hazard to the people exposed to it. The exact scope of this potential health hazard is impossible to accurately quantify at this time . . . . Unfortunately, the real answer to the problem will not be available until some ten to twenty years from this date when the health experience of those exposed to the fibers emitted from Reserve's plant is reviewed . . . . Under no circumstances will the Court allow the people of Duluth to be continuously and indefinitely exposed to a known human carcinogen in order that the people in Silver Bay can continue working at their jobs . . . . Defendants have the economic and engineering capability to carry out an on-land disposal system that satisfies the health and environmental considerations raised. For reasons unknown to this Court they have chosen not to implement such a plan. In essence they have decided to continue exposing thousands daily to a substantial health risk in order to maintain the current profitability of the present operation and delay the capital outlay . . . needed to institute modifications. The Court has

Aerial view of one of Reserve Mining's chutes dumping tailings (see back cover)

no other alternative but to order an immediate halt to the discharge which threatens the lives of thousands.[14]

The decision to close the plant immediately (12:01 A.M., April 21, 1974) was a very dramatic one, and it highlighted Judge Lord's determination that the company comply with the law. However, two days later, after Reserve appealed to a higher court, three judges met in St. Louis, Missouri, and ruled that the plant could reopen while appeals were made. In June, 1974, that same panel of judges, after further study, demanded that Reserve present plans for future on-land disposal. So the legal battle continues, as appeals to higher courts are made and plans for on-land disposal are discussed.

Although both the three-judge panel and Judge Miles Lord ruled that Reserve should stop dumping, there was an important difference in their reasoning. Judge Lord based his order on the threat of a potential health hazard. The panel of judges rejected this, because illness as a result of the dumping had not been proved. They instead named general pollution of the lake as the offense. This is a significant distinction, and one which should be resolved as the case moves up through the courts, perhaps to the Supreme Court eventually. Citizens point out, however, that *every day* of delay, as trials and appeals go on, Reserve continues to deposit 67,000 tons of the tailings into Lake Superior.

In the fall of 1975 the circuit court disagreed with Judge Lord on another issue, namely his handling of payment for temporary drinking water filtration for North Shore residents. Judge Lord insisted Reserve should be responsible. The court appointed Judge Edward J. Devitt to succeed Miles Lord in November, 1975. Judge

Devitt immediately ruled that Reserve must pay costs for water filtration.

On May 4, 1976, Reserve Mining Company was fined more than one million dollars for violating state water permits and "willfully delaying a final resolution" of the court case. Judge Devitt's ruling backed Judge Lord's original decisions against Reserve, most importantly in agreeing that the dumping of taconite wastes constitutes a cancer-producing threat to public health. Reserve chose to appeal the decision.

Unfortunately, Judge Devitt did not set a deadline for determining a site and method of on-land disposal, and while this and the appeal are being decided Reserve's tailings continue to pour into the lake. (Since this book was first printed in December, 1974, more than thirty-five million tons of tailings have been dumped by Reserve Mining Company into Lake Superior.)

The struggle has lasted for eight years, and until Reserve's wastes are disposed of on land it will not have ended. But, as Martin Lindquist, an elderly gentleman from Herbster, Wisconsin, said at a past annual meeting of the SLSA, none of what has been accomplished will be of any value if young people who care about Lake Superior do not continue to work for the cause. He said young people have what he does not — time. Reserve can afford to stall. So can other companies. Only if young people keep a constant watch over Lake Superior for years to come, will we be able to feel secure about its future.

8.

THE
PRESENT

The future of Lake Superior is of concern to everyone, and not just to those who live on its shores. Both the United States and Canadian governments are coming to realize the unique value of Superior, and are seeking ways of protecting it. However, even now, serious threats to the lake are taking form. For example, because the levels of the lower Great Lakes are rising, the U.S. Army Corps of Engineers wants to use Lake Superior as a reservoir, holding back some of its water by closing the locks at Sault Sainte Marie. This, however, would raise the level of Lake Superior considerably and cause enormous changes along the shoreline, many of which scientists cannot even predict. To tamper with the level of the lake is a dangerous operation, and much research

Twenty-seven vessels stuck in the ice at the entrance of Duluth's harbor after an April blizzard in 1924

should be done before it is seriously considered. The Army Corps is already raising the level to some extent, however, on an "emergency basis." Many citizens have complained that their shoreline is seriously eroding.

Another instance of tampering with nature's ways is shown in the Army Corp's plans to try keeping the port of Duluth-Superior open all winter long. Right now the port is frozen in from about December until late March. There are various possible methods of keeping it open, but the Corps is experimenting at present with piping air along the harbor bottom through plastic tunnels. As the bubbles rise to the surface, the warmer bottom water circulates to the top, preventing ice from forming, or melting ice that has already formed. This plan will have a definite effect on the ecology of the lake, altering plant and animal life by changing temperatures and stirring up bottom sediment. Also, citizens are questioning the logic of allowing oil tankers, which have been known to break up from just rough waters during a storm, to move around on a lake that will have floating chunks of ice on it.

Another issue, which has split many of the citizen groups, is that of building a superhighway along the lake's North Shore in Minnesota. Right now, Highway 61, which is a two-lane road, follows that route. An undoubtedly safer and much wider multilane highway has been proposed, but it has raised questions of aesthetics, economics, and safety. Many of the tourist towns feel the highway will encourage business by making the lake much more accessible. Others worry about additional people, cars, and boats, and about the visual effect of the road itself, not to mention the noise and air pollution caused by automobiles.

All of these issues raise important questions which we must try to answer. To what extent have people the right to change nature for their convenience? Isn't it possible that nature will react in ways we cannot anticipate to foil our plans, and perhaps to cause us to regret such interference? How important are economic progress and technical convenience in comparison with nature's complicated balance? If we destroy that balance will we ultimately destroy ourselves? To what extent should a natural "resource" such as Lake Superior be something man "uses" and to what extent should it be considered something valuable in itself, to be left alone and respected?

If we agree that man must, to survive, change the land

somewhat to serve his economic purposes, where do we draw the line? Where do we say "enough"? When is it too late?

These questions should make us realize how much we all owe to groups such as the Save Lake Superior Association. They are looking for answers to these questions. They are seeking ways for citizens to make balanced, educated decisions about the future of Lake Superior. They know that the decisions citizens make now will affect the future of the lake for hundreds of years to come.

Without such groups as the SLSA, many beautiful areas of the United States would have been destroyed by man. As it is, in the case of Lake Superior, we are almost too late. We can only hope that the damage which has been done can be repaired in time. And we, as citizens, can give groups such as this support — both in time and in donations — so that they can carry on their important work.

9.

THE
FUTURE

This book has attempted to give a general view of the environmental problems of Lake Superior, and to show how these problems developed in the context of the geology, industrial development, and political climate of the region.

If the story of the people's battle with environmental problems, especially in the case of the Reserve Mining Company, teaches us nothing else, it should demonstrate that in our system of government, it is the *citizens,* and not just their elected officials, who must ultimately accept the responsibility of being guardians of the land. Men and women in government are only human, and their values do not always accurately reflect those of the state or nation as a whole. Officials may, for example, feel that a growing and prospering industry is more important to the welfare of a town, or state, or nation, than the environmental quality of that area. The people may disagree. It is up to the citizens, and that means *you* and *me,* to express their views on such an issue, and to do this consistently.

As we have seen, this is not an easy task. We must learn patience, persistence, and determination. We cannot always win a debate overnight. But we must not give up because of temporary frustrations or one or two defeats. These are part of the political process, and we must keep trying.

It is our responsibility to speak and act to see that a magnificent natural resource such as Lake Superior is not destroyed for hundreds of years to come by the thoughtless actions of a few people. Look around you, where you live. Is there a beautiful marsh, full of wild flowers, birds, and underwater creatures, soon to be filled in for the construction of a shopping center or a highway? Is there a small grove of trees to be torn down for an apartment building? Will a highrise be built on the banks of a wild and lovely river?

Whether or not these things happen depends largely upon how the citizens of the area react. If you are one of those citizens, are you going to get involved?

NOTES

1. United States Department of the Interior, Federal Water Pollution Control Administration, *Proceedings, Conference on (the) Pollution of Lake Superior and its Tributary Basin, Minnesota-Wisconsin-Michigan, May 13-14-15, 1969*, pp. 1498-1499.

2. *Collections of the Minnesota Historical Society*, Volume III (St. Paul: Minnesota Historical Society, 1880), p. 334.

3. Louis Agassiz, *Lake Superior: Its Physical Character, Vegetation and Animals* (Boston: Gould, Kendal and Lincoln, 1850. Reprinted, New York Times, 1970), p. 34.

4. Ibid., p. 62.

5. *Collections of the Minnesota Historical Society*, p. 339.

6. Ibid., p. 342.

7. Grace Lee Nute, *Lake Superior* (Indianapolis: Bobbs-Merrill, 1944), p. 132.

8. Stanley Ulrich et al., *Superior Polluter* (Duluth: Save Lake Superior Association and Northern Environmental Council, 1972), p. 12.

9. United States Department of the Interior, Federal Water Pollution Control Administration, *Proceedings . . . May 13-14-15, 1969*, p. 328.

10. Ibid., p. 735.

11. Ibid., p. 743.

12. Ibid., p. 1067.

13. Ibid., p. 1463.

14. United States District Court, District of Minnesota, Fifth Division, *Memorandum and Order*. United States of America et al., Plaintiffs v. Reserve Mining Company et al., Defendants. April 20, 1974.

GLOSSARY

algae. Groups of very simple plants, without true leaves or stems, generally living in water

asbestosis. A fibrous hardening of the lungs occurring among people exposed to asbestos

carcinogen. Any substance that tends to produce cancer

clear-cutting. The process of cutting all trees in a given area (for lumber) rather than cutting them selectively, leaving the younger ones to continue to grow

ecology. The interrelationships of living things and their environments, or the study of such interrelationships

effluent. Gases or liquids, in some instances containing pollutants, cast into the surrounding environment

flush-out time. Time a body of water takes to replenish itself

"green water" effect. The green color resulting when a lake is overfertilized by nutrients which produce more organic matter than the water's self-purification process can overcome.

iron range. Any large deposit of iron in the earth's surface

mesothelioma. Cancer of the pleura, which is the membrane that encases the lungs, or the peritoneum, which is the membrane that lines the stomach

silt. Very fine loose sand carried by moving or running water and deposited as sediment

taconite. A hard rock containing about 30 percent iron in the form of fine specks of iron oxide

tailings. The residues from the processing of any product, especially in the mining of ores

turbidity. Cloudiness of water or air, as when it is muddied with particles or other foreign matter

BIBLIOGRAPHY

Agassiz, Louis. *Lake Superior: Its Physical Character, Vegetation and Animals.* Boston: Gould, Kendal and Lincoln, 1850. Reprinted, New York Times, 1970.
This gives a firsthand account of what Lake Superior looked like over one hundred years ago.

Brodeur, Paul. *Asbestos and Enzymes.* New York: Ballantine, 1972.
The first half of this book contains an excellent history of the relationship between asbestos and health, describing the difficulty with which the effects of asbestos were first traced, and explaining the various physical symptoms and diseases caused directly or indirectly by the substance. The rest of the book discusses laundry detergent enzymes.

Heilbron, Gertha L. *The Thirty Second State: A Pictorial History of Minnesota.* St. Paul: Minnesota Historical Society, 1966.
The author of this book traveled all over the Midwest, collecting hundreds of photographs, maps, paintings, and drawings which depict the history of Minnesota. These illustrations are accompanied by a very clearly written history of the state. It's fun to see what Lake Superior looked like in the 1800s, and to get a look at the voyageurs' huge canoes.

Mengel, J. T. *Geology of the Western Lake Superior.* Superior, Wisconsin: Geology Department, Wisconsin State University, 1970.
Mengel tells how this area of Superior was formed, in words the layman can understand. This would be particularly interesting to read before or after a visit to the Duluth-Superior area.

Nute, Grace Lee. *Lake Superior*. Indianapolis: Bobbs-Merrill Co., 1944.

Although this book is over thirty years old, it is probably the most comprehensive history of the lake yet written.

Poatgeiter, A. Hermina, and Dunn, James Taylor, editors, *Gopher Reader*. St. Paul: Minnesota Historical Society and Minnesota Statehood Centennial Commission, 1958.

This is a compilation of over one hundred articles on Minnesota taken from issues of *Gopher Historian,* which was a publication for young people. The articles are fascinating, as are the many old photographs and drawings, most taken from the files of the Minnesota Historical Society.

Steinhacker, Charles. *Superior*. New York: Harper & Row, 1971.

If you wondered whether or not Lake Superior is as beautiful as its admirers say, you won't have any doubts after looking at this volume of color photographs. Steinhacker captures the lake's many moods and the variety of surrounding terrain.

Ulrich, Stanley; Berg, Timothy J.; and Hedlund, Deborah. *Superior Polluter*. Duluth: Save Lake Superior Association and Northern Environmental Council, 1972.

This is the only fairly complete account of the early development of the Reserve Mining case. Although somewhat technical, it is worth reading for a good understanding of the issues.

United States Department of the Interior, Federal Water Pollution Control Administration. *Proceedings, Conference on (the) Pollution of Lake Superior and Its Tributary Basin, Minnesota-Wisconsin-Michigan, May 13-14-15, 1969.*

The conference proceedings are hundreds of pages long, but they are certainly worth reading selectively, as there is much to learn from the testimony of the various individuals.

United States Environmental Protection Agency. *Guidelines for Developing or Revising Water Quality Standards Under the Federal Water Pollution Control Act Amendments of 1972.* Washington, D.C.: U. S. Government Printing Office, 1973.

Here is just one example of the many government documents which could give background information helpful to a study of Lake Superior's problems. It explains how local governments can implement federal water pollution control laws.

THE AUTHOR
Wendy Wriston Adamson earned
a bachelor's degree in political
science from Syracuse University
in 1964, and a master's degree
in library science from Simmons
College in 1971. The following
year she helped set up and staff
the Environmental Conservation
Library within the Minneapolis
Public Library. Since 1972, Ms.
Adamson has been a librarian at
the Environmental Library of
Minnesota.

*The photographs are reproduced through the courtesy of the
Duluth Convention and Visitors Bureau, Duluth Public Library,
Environmental Protection Agency Documerica, Earl Johnson,
Grant Merritt, Minneapolis Public Library, Minnesota Depart-
ment of Natural Resources, National Water Quality Laboratory,
Reserve Mining Company, and St. Louis County Historical
Society.*